LOVE

the feel-good factor

LOVE
the feel-good factor

Libby Willis
Illustrated by Debbie Lush

**Andrews McMeel
Publishing**

Kansas City

introduction

Love is in the air. It surrounds us in a million songs, films, pictures, and books. But we never run out of fresh things to say about it, new ways to celebrate and express it. Love is an enigma with endless variations.

Everyone is created for love. Everyone is lovable. Experiencing love, giving and receiving love, and sustaining love are central to our existence. And love is the greatest influence on who we are, defining our identity.

Love can surprise us out of the blue and send us somersaulting, turning our world upside down. Or it can slowly, secretly grow until one day we suddenly see it standing there strong and soaring as a sequoia. Love is magical and mystical, whisking us away into an enchanted world made just for two, where time stands still and every flower seems to bloom, every lark seems to sing, purely for us. It is a whirlwind, a waltz, yet also the still point at the center where two souls circle each other in silent slow motion, moving shyly closer until two become wondrously one.

Elated, exalted, we float above rooftops, we swing from chandeliers to our special serenade. Love makes poets, composers, artists of us all. Love is the elixir of life. It transfigures us, and all we look at, bathing the world in a halo of golden light.

And someone whom the world deems dull and ordinary becomes in our eyes the most extraordinary person in the universe. That they should love us too seems the greatest miracle of all.

Yet love is so much more than the fairy-tale wonder of "Once upon a time…" It is the even more wonderful reality of the ever after.

It is the enriching and perfecting of two people as their love grows and deepens year by year. It stretches us, making us the best we can be, our best self—yet at the same time it makes us utterly selfless.

Love overflows. From loving a single person, our hearts expand to love a multitude of other people; like a rose-quartz pebble dropped in a pond, it sends out ripples of love in ever-increasing circles. Love links parent and child, friend and friend, owner and pet. And with the grace of spiritual love we encounter the divine.

Love is feeling and being, but it is equally doing. It is thinking of the one we love, truly listening, endlessly and joyfully giving. It is the marvel of finding that, however much we give, more still bubbles up within us. That, however wonderful it is to receive love, it is even more so to give it. That loving others blesses our life with meaning.

That loving is the most important thing we do in our lives. We give up everything for love, and find we are rich beyond our dreams.

Love lifts us up to hover with angels, yet it reaches down to our lowest depths of need. Love is our life jacket when tragedies, pain, and grief capsize us. We say that we fall in love, but really we climb into it: Love is our stairway to heaven.

Loving is the answer to all the big questions in life. It colors and permeates everything; it is our splendor and our glory. It is the wisdom of the old couple, the trusting innocence of the little child. Its mystery, intimacy, immensity, intensity are beyond our understanding. But ultimately it does not matter that we do not understand it. All that matters is that we love. For love is in essence sublimely simple. To live is to love; to love is to live.

a garden is a lovesome thing

Love is the gentle art of hearticulture. Its favorite flowers are the old-fashioned sort, such as cheerfulness, honesty, and forget-me-nots. Given time and space to be themselves and blossom and grow as nature intended; bedded down well and talked to, regularly watered and supported, they will bloom year after year. It is wise to be watchful for weeds, and to remember the value of regular pruning, trimming away the little disagreements and irritations that spoil and wither love. But gently does it: the sheer bliss of topiary comes from tiny tweaks, not cutting remarks. An allotment, too, can teach us a lot about love: to use the carrot rather than the stick; not to rake over old arguments, but to lay on loyalty with a trowel. Love will reward us in spades.

jean therapy

Love, like a beloved pair of jeans we have worn day in, day out, so they hug our every contour, can suddenly fall apart at the seams. Tempers, like hems, can fray; patience, like denim, wear thin; communication, like zippers, break down. But tender loving care, patching up, and a lot of time and attention can make things

better than new. We can never have the art of love all sewn up—it takes a lifetime to learn—but that is part of its appeal. Customizing our love as we go along, creating a bespoke affair tailor-made for two, is a project with infinite possibilities. Add sequin kisses and rejoice that in love we are meant to be pair-shaped.

silence is golden

Like the viola, love values the virtues that belong to muted things. We love, the poets say, "to the level of every day's / Most quiet need, by sun and candlelight." Love is not so much never having to say you're sorry as never having to say anything. We treasure every "close-companioned inarticulate hour / When twofold silence was the song of love." A squeeze of a hand, an invitation in the eyes, or a hug, can be more eloquent than any words. In silent stillness two souls surrender to each other in complete communion and rest in perfect peace.

if the gap fits

Love is no respecter of ages. It takes age gaps in its stride and skips to and fro from May to September, September to May. Love runs rings round rules and mores, for the heart is nothing if not unconventional. Marriages made in heaven are founded on true affinities, which do not always fit nicely into accepted norms of what is suitable. They only gain in strength from defying predictions that they will not last. Love is an exuberant designer that delights in juxtaposing the old with the new, vintage with contemporary. The secret lies in the mix. It has an unerring instinct for fresh combinations that infuse both pieces with original charm: a twenties bag with a sixties strap, a forties jacket with a seventies belt, with love's sure touch become genuine classics.

river deep, mountain high

Love bubbles up as a spring high in the Blue Ridge Mountains. It streams over pebbles, translucent and showered with golden coins of sunlight falling through emerald leaves. As it widens into a river it flows through ever-changing landscapes. It tumbles down waterfalls and races over rapids, meanders through sleepy meadows and winds through wildernesses. It changes course and direction but is always heading toward the sea. It is not always taking soundings of its depths or measuring its breadth. It does not judge its dimensions. It has its own intrinsic integrity. Our love may sometimes be choppy and troubled on the surface, sometimes still and tranquil. But little by little it is always widening, deepening, maturing; always following its star.

loving and giving

What can we give to the one who has everything except the love we long to give them, the love they may not even suspect suffuses our heart? If it is a lucky gift, one that touches the loved one to acceptance by its sensitivity and thoughtfulness, we can sometimes be gathered in along with it, like the tail of a kite being ever so slowly, ever so carefully, reeled in. And there we are.

making tracks

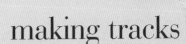

It can happen. Once in a while we meet love on our very first outing. But mostly we have a long list of liaisons that we play again and again in our minds, like tracks on an old LP, each with its unforgettable score. Some fast and furious, electrifying; some slowburning, lush, and hypnotic; others bittersweet blues. Yet each is important as a stage in our development and imparts a special message. All contribute a phrase or a chord to the composition of our true anthem. And in time that standout song will come, so achingly perfect in every note that the hairs on the back of our neck stand up and we know that this is the platinum one.

love's lifeline

The rubber band of love is fantastically elastic. There seems no limit to what it can encompass. It embraces failure as well as success, interfering in-laws and finicky friends. It expands to make room for a houseful of guests and encourages a whole host of hobbies, finding space for trainsets and treadmills, motorcycles and massive zucchinis. Love goes around the lumpy moments of grumpiness and makes allowances for angry words. It extends to accommodate a spreading girth and responds to stretch marks with sympathy. It holds things together faithfully when they feel on the verge of falling apart.

to love and to cherish

Love may claim it is as tough as old boots or has a rhinoceros hide. But even old boots need a polish now and then, and rhinoceroses respond to stroking. Love is resilient but nevertheless it needs to be cherished. The harder we love, the harder hurts hurt. It is fearfully easy to take love for granted. Yet a little gesture or just a few words can do so much, especially on uneasy or monotonous days. Like the dab of perfume on a wrist when spirits are flagging.

lost and found

No search and rescue team is more tireless than love. It will crawl down to the deepest cave, climb the most dangerous crevasse. It is our life buoy when we are drowning, our safety net when we are falling, our parachute when we have to bail out. It is the shepherd of a hundred sheep who will not sleep when a lamb is lost until he has found and returned it to the fold. Love lassoes us to life and will never let us go.

a close-knit couple

The pattern can seem simple when we first begin, but then our attention wanders or enthusiasm ebbs and before we know it there are mistakes in the relationship we longed to knit. But we need not despair or give up. The wonderful thing about love is that it is endlessly resourceful and revels in rescue jobs. Like necessity, it is the mother of invention. It gets you through the tricky patches by stimulating creativity. You don't have to follow a pattern—make up your own, turning the holes that resulted from misunderstandings into quirky design features. And don't worry if it seems to be on the XXXL size: A love affair is meant to be big enough and cozy enough to keep you both warm.

loving cup

Mixology can seem a hard art to master, but with dedication everyone can become a maestro of love's heartwarming cocktail. Take:

2 measures trust
1 measure commitment
1 measure friendship
¾ measure understanding
⅔ measure patience
1 dash laughter
1 teaspoon romance

Blend well together, pour out a generous glassful, and serve stirred, not shaken. Sprinkle with kisses, and top with a slice of passion fruit.

the sky's the limit

Shall we compare love to a summer's day? It is more lovely and more temperate, for its eternal summer does not fade. On a day spent together at the seaside, love is the golden sand beneath bare feet, soft as silk yet firm forever. It is the sun that smiles its beams upon us. It is the tide that tenderly laps the shore, ebbing and flowing unfailingly. It dances with a pair of seahorses that bond for life. It sends heartstopping waves to surf together, and scatters starfish to wish upon. It builds breakwaters for safety and security, sandcastles to let us dream dreams. It whisks us up on a Ferris wheel for those cloud-touching treats that refresh a relationship, then brings us gently down to earth again.

terms of endearment

Even if we had as many words for love as Eskimos have for snow, they could never convey its every nuance. But everyone can learn the language of love, however tongue-tied they are. It needs no interpreter. Love is an action verb, the giving of time, of thought, of self. Its favorite prepositions are "with" and "for." For pronouns it uses "you" far more than "I;" it prefers "There you are" to "Here I am." It is a dialogue, not a monologue. It stutters over polysyllables, but its simple, heartfelt sentences express eternal truths. And sometimes all we need to say is "Read my lips."

question time

How do we know it's the Real McCoy? It's the million-dollar question. A million dollars focus the mind, but heart and soul need to focus too. Will we still love when there is more of the worse than the better, more of the poorer than the richer, more of the sickness than the health? Love is a deep, undying certainty that we want to be together through everything: the highs and the lows and the just so-sos. But total certainty is often not there at the start—we can be beset by butterflies of doubt even as we say yes. The only way to reach it is to set out on the road that leads toward it. "You stand at the crossroads of the path of love and the path of fear. Which do you choose to follow?"

random hearts

Love tiptoes up from behind and taps us on the shoulder when we least expect it. We can meet it in places where we absolutely knew we would never find it. Book clubs can be a disappointment, for love is stranger than fiction, and supermarket singles sessions can leave us with a freezer full of French fries. Yet dullmen.com could yield a rich seam of rough diamonds. The man who gets high on watching paint dry and has a degree in doughnut dunking may well share our passion for Play-Doh and pogo sticks. Love broadens the mind and breaks down our preconceptions. Love can spring up on the most unpromising sites.

unexpected treasures

Love rarely turns out how we thought it would. But if it seldom corresponds to our dreams, we are often left with richer realities. Illusions may fade away like the ink on love letters found in a trunk; hopes may crumble into a sad heap of dust. The lover we worshipped turns out to be flawed and far removed from the hero of our fantasies. But with the maturity and wisdom of years lived together can come a truer appreciation of the work of art that has been created by all the days of little interactions, of give and take

and simple satisfactions. In a sudden flash of joyful insight we can suddenly see that, just as marble may be made out of scraps of mortar, glass and pebbles, so out of quirks, foibles and human failings may be fashioned a love that will stand the test of time and gleam with the beauty of solidity.

there's no accounting for love

Love would make a poor accountant. It doesn't bother with balance sheets. It makes a huge investment—all it has to give—but doesn't demand a return. It shares its life savings with a joyful heart and, when even more is called for, digs deep in its pockets to offer its last mite. It lends again and again without charging interest and forgives not seven times but seventy times seven.

Money worries can lead to tensions and eat into our fund of affection—one person may be a big spender, the other a rainy-day hoarder. But problems can be solved with

communication and honesty. Possession
plays no part in true love: Seeking to own our
lover completely makes them feel trapped and
can let jealousy invade our hearts. Total trust brings
gilt-edged security—we can enjoy each other's
freedom and independence, and feel no need to
keep a strict tally of how much time or
love is given to other people. We know
that in each other we have someone we
can always bank on.

ladder of love

Love smiles at our superstitions. We may try to conjure it with spells and potions, charms and runes, but love will enchant us in its own wise way, more real and sustaining than a sprig of mistletoe. Love cannot be second-guessed; it knows better than we do who will make us happy. It is when we are headstrong and override our intuition that we leap into unsuitable relationships. If we are heartstrong instead, letting love take the reins, it will lead us in its own good time to our rightful love. So, when the mirror of our fantasies shatters on Friday the 13th, it is not the end of the world: Love may well bump into us under a ladder.

music of the heart

No one can sit down at a piano for the first time and play a concerto. It takes hours of patient practice, of persevering with our scales so that we can master the complex passages. Love, too, will have its high notes and low notes, its chords and discords. Living through the caprices of day-to-day routine helps us negotiate tricky intervals. We delight in discovering hidden harmonies, feeling into the piece, noting the changes of key. We find that a duet played appassionato is a confetti of grace notes. And we learn that in love, as in music, the silences between the notes are as meaningful as the sounds.

balancing act

Symmetrical features are said to be seductive, attracting us to a potential partner. Some couples seem to grow more like each other, as pets do their owners, even finishing each other's sentences. But love in reality is rarely balanced. We cannot align it with a spirit level or make it equal with scales. There will almost always be differences in lovers' degree of desire and commitment. Moods and feelings are bound to seesaw with the pressures and problems of life. But none of this need matter, as long as we are prepared for it and accept it as natural. Through give and take our relationship will find its own happy equilibrium.

the wings of love

If love alights on us like a fledgling dove, we should let it rest awhile, feeling the kiss of its creamy wings on our skin. Still and calm, we are soothed by its quiet cooing. If it flies away, to wheel upon the softest breezes and skim the tops of apple trees, we should let it. If it returns, it has chosen us. If not, it was not meant to be and it has found another dovecote. But, because we gave it its freedom, did not try to keep it in a gilded cage, the love intended for us will arrive one day quite out of the blue and make its nest in our heart.

don't go changing

Misfit does not feature in love's lexicon. Love accepts us as we are or as we may become. Love delights in the love we offer, not asking it to be other: It knows that, however hard it tries, a pear tree cannot produce plums nor a Manx cat twirl a tail. Love dispenses with the three Rs of recriminations, resentments, and reproaches. It does not question or give the third degree. Love does not force us to change but supports us when we seek to change ourselves. Love forgives all. Far from being judge and jury, love is always our defense counsel; even when we have hurt it, love pleads a long list of mitigating factors and never finds us guilty.

the things we do for love

There is no greater inspiration than love. For love, we promise perilous things. For love, we achieve them. Love stretches us to our full potential and coaxes us out of our comfort zone. We dare to do the dangerous, attempt the impossible, defy the odds, cross the deserts. We roller coaster side by side on a white-knuckle ride from the sublime to the ridiculous. We skydive together holding hands, spread-eagled amid the clouds, careless of where the currents carry us. Love makes us megawatt, turbo-charged, jet-propelled. We risk everything for love, for nothing else matters.

a many-splendored thing

A miraculous aspect of love is that there are not just fifty-seven varieties; there are an infinite number. Each of us feels different kinds of love for different things: We love our cat, we love tulips, we love playing the oboe, we love dancing, we love denim. On another level we love the land we farm, the job we do, the natural world.

Higher, or deeper, still we feel spiritual love. From that central maypole love fans out countless other interweaving loves, for all the people we cherish in subtly different ways: our soul mate, our children, parents, sisters, brothers, grandparents, friends. Love comes in a limitless stream of shapes, sizes, textures, and strengths.

circus act

Can you hear the cry of the popcorn vendor, feel the sawdust beneath your feet, see the ringmaster's ruby-red coat? Love summons all the skills of the circus: the practice put into the juggling act, the sense of humor of the clowns, the balance of the tightrope walker, the trust of the trapeze artist

in her partner, the intuition of the mind reader,
the gentleness of the lion tamer. Life under
the big top is a spectacular affair,
throbbing with thrills and spills.
It is love big time.

the color of love

What color is love? For people with the condition known as synesthesia, numbers and letters pulsate with color, so *2* may be orange and *3* pink, *u* may be green and *i* red, and *a* have the look of weathered wood. How do we see our love? Is it turquoise as a Seychelles tide, lapping the toes of two who lie side by side on silken sand, an ankle overlapping an ankle? Is it white as the Taj Mahal at noon, as the unicorn in the forest clearing? Is it red as an armful of laughing roses, as a ruby slipped on a faithful finger? Is it yellow as the haystack of first flushed kisses? A "mad magenta moment" on a barge of purple perfumed sails? Or is it indelible indigo, when green and yellow blend to blue on a dyed cloth lifted into the oxygen of love?

head over heels

Sometimes, for fear of being left on the shelf, we force ourselves into something we pretend is love. But an ill-fitting pair of shoes, however much admired and must-have, will only do us harm, hurting and distorting. It takes courage to walk away from a love affair that we know deep down is wrong, but staying will mean even more pain for both. However much we fear being single, it can prove liberating to go footloose and fancy free for a while, so that we feel the grass beneath our feet and dance barefoot in the park. We find that we can cope on our own, can make our own decisions; we discover strengths we never suspected we had. So that the next time we stumble upon love, knowing ourselves better, we will know if we have found our soul mate.

plain sailing

We can be sailing along smoothly through life, then all of a sudden have a sinking feeling and find we are seriously adrift. We may even be perilously close to the rocks. Cherished plans come to nothing, relationships disintegrate, trust is betrayed. Usually it is partly our fault and partly other people's fault. Love may be trying to tell us something, so perhaps we should look inside ourselves to find where we have been going wrong. Perhaps, unknowingly, we have been battling against the current. Why not let love take control? If we accept life's natural flow and let ourselves be borne along, love will steer us around the rocks and carry us where we are meant to go. We can still keep hold of the tiller, but just nudge it gently, relaxing into the river, going with the flow. Not knowing exactly where we are heading is part of the adventure. Trust that love will float your boat.

that healing feeling

Lavender, rose, ylang ylang, juniper, ginger, chamomile: Love is the best essential oil. It does the work of all the others. It purifies and cleanses, soothes away stresses and tensions, and eases an aching heart. It relaxes and restores, refreshes and rejuvenates. It stimulates the mind and uplifts downcast spirits. Love is a greater healer than time. Love ministers to a bruised pride and when we have fallen flat on our faces it never says, "I told you so." Love is there when we wake from a nightmare, wills us back to life from a coma. Love gives the kiss of life to a stranger.

a little goes a long way

Once upon a time there was a king who had a beautiful and beloved daughter. Two rich suitors came to the palace, seeking her hand in marriage. To test them, the king said that the strap of one of her favorite shoes had broken and she needed a safety pin to hold it together. One of the suitors, thinking this was a trick and that the king actually wanted a son-in-law who would keep his daughter in luxury, went off and after quite some time returned bearing a shoebox tower of swanky satin sandals. The other came back much sooner, with just a safety pin. The king declared that he would give the princess to the one who had brought the pin: "The one who cares for her in little things is the one who really cares." In love, it does not matter if we cannot provide expensive presents or grand gestures; in love, it is truly the thought that counts.

the nearness of you

Distance is no obstacle to love. In the ocean depths blue whales send sonic serenades across thousands of sonar miles. When two hearts are apart, they are still indissolubly joined, just as "twin compasses are two," separated to trace out different circles yet never doubting they will be reunited. Love is so loyal that it does not need to be present to prove it. Love knows that moments of aloneness refresh and reinforce it; it passes the surest test "for a bond between two people: that each protects the solitude of the other."

young at heart

Autumn's misty sunlight falls soft on the old gold of a ring burnished by sixty summers. From their veranda rocking chairs the folks who live on the hill look back across the valley, with tender eyes retracing the lanes of memory they have walked through hand in hand. Love only improves with age. It is mellow and hallowed as vintage wine. It is known in its inmost secret places, yet still has treasures to vouchsafe. It is a painting on the wall that we look at daily, seeing something new in it with every viewing. It is a novel read and reread many times, yet ever surprising us with insights we had overlooked. The passing years bring joy, not fear: For those who love, time is eternity.

as good as new

No matter how eagerly we set off on a love affair, bright-eyed and bushy-tailed, at some stage we start to feel we are living in a Groundhog Day. We say the same things, have the same disagreements, do the same mundane tasks, get stuck in humdrum routines. Which is a shame, as love is a wondrous, priceless thing, too precious to let it dwindle to being simply part of the furniture. But love responds well to pampering. We can revitalize it in a hundred little ways: going to new places together, or revisiting ones that hold special memories; doing new things together, or doing again things we did when we first met; or not doing but simply being, spending time alone in mystical intimacy. Then every morning will seem like the first morning, sparkling with the first dewfall on the first grass.

perfect timing

Does love wear a watch? Probably not. It has a well-earned reputation for arriving at inconvenient moments. Yet love knows the meaning of time more truly than we do. "Time is our choice of how to love and why." We know that a day with a lover seems gone in a minute but time apart is like one hundred years of solitude. Even so, sometimes we

squander time together, or let other demands ration us to a handful of snatched seconds. Love is not to be found by rushing on to a receding future or pining for an air-brushed past. Love is here in the present moment, if we can live truly, richly, deeply in it, soaking in it like a warm bath, embracingly bubbly and soul-restoring.

measure for measure

If we measure out our love with coffee spoons, we end up with espressos: short, intense shots to the heart that leave us restless and jittery, forever confused and searching. If we lavish it out with ladles, we will drink deeply of

a long and nourishing relationship, frothy with the milk of human kindness, sustaining in its special blend of companionship and constancy. Love is an overflowing cup: The more we give away, the more we have to give.

the food of love

It has been said that "All that matters in a relationship is that you like the same pizza toppings." Food can certainly test our tact in love. When love's labors are lost in the oven, a long-awaited dinner emerging hours late, charred, shriveled and hard as a rock, how will we react? When the kitchen looks like a paintball zone, will we roll up our sleeves, pull on the dishwashing gloves, and tackle the blackened lasagne pan? When the dog has wolfed down the sirloin steak, will we send for a takeout? We can plan an aphrodisiac feast of oysters, asparagus and chocolate mousse, but every meal can be lip-smacking when prepared and served with love. True fusion food—the daily nourishing of a relationship with kindness and kisses—outlasts all trends. Love is always the flavor of the month.

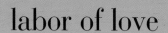

labor of love

How do all the essential
chores that no one really wants to do
somehow do themselves by magic? Miraculously,
overnight, a pile of shirts will appear from nowhere,
laundered and ironed immaculately. Soggy towels levitate from
the bathroom floor and return in fluffily clean condition. Missing
socks materialize and muddy footprints vanish. Leaves disappear

from blocked-up drains and greasemarks from stoves. There is always fresh fruit in the bowl, the refrigerator is never empty, and the toothpaste never runs out. Love takes on the thankless, easily forgotten tasks. Invisibly, without a word, it shows itself in actions.

rest assured

We may read every book about love, analyze it to the nth degree and put it under a microscope, but still be no closer to knowing what it is. The solution may be simply to love, like a newborn baby that doesn't intellectualize but instinctively knows it needs love and responds to the love it receives. An ounce of love is worth a pound of knowledge. If we feel like a tennis ball being hit back and forth endlessly, perhaps we should abandon asking whether it is a right relationship or a wrong relationship and accept with joy that it is our relationship. And then just take things one day at a time, playing to each other's strengths and working on our own faults. The result of a perfect match is love all.

where the heart is

Where is love? Is it the oak porch of an ancient church as the light fades on a winter's afternoon, where time stands still and all creation holds its breath, to hear the answer to a whispered question? Is it under the wings of an alabaster angel, where raindrops glisten on the petals of freshly picked pansies laid by a tiny headstone? Or is it the sacred place where two souls meet in total peace, where secrets are told, confessions made, hopes and fears revealed, where we face ourselves in all our frailty and are transfigured by the unconditional radiance reflected back to us?

what lies beneath

Each love affair is deliciously intriguing and tantalizing to outsiders. Only two people know its secrets. A couple who seem tempestuous in public may be tranquil when alone together; two who seem placid and prosaic may explode into passion behind closed doors. Each relationship is a unique organism with its own complex DNA, which it can take a lifetime to unravel. Each is a foreign, hidden world whose buried treasures, rich resources, and breathtaking landscapes only two explorers will ever discover, charting it side by side.

topsy-turvy

Love can be incredibly messy. It may blow in and overturn all our preconceptions, sweep treasured priorities from the mantel, and throw our cushioned existence into disarray. If we feel disturbed by this and try to contain it, to fold it up neatly to lie in a drawer and take out only on special occasions, love may be trying to tell us something. To loosen up, let go, live a little on the wild side. To see that life is too short to line up our lupines with a ruler. To throw away the rule book and do cartwheels on the lawn.

wait and see

The right person does not have to be pursued. Love, like the wind, blows where it will; it cannot be caught in a butterfly net. If we go out hunting for love it will bound away frightened into the forest and hide amid the foliage. If we wait at the edge of the forest, quiet and patient and simply looking with welcoming eyes, love will be intrigued. Slowly, diffidently, it will draw toward us and nuzzle its way into our heart.

slowly but surely

Love in the fast lane feels fantastic at first. Rushing along at top speed, we can miss warning signs, take wrong turns, and have only a hazy impression of where we are heading—until we come to a shuddering halt and realize we have been on a road to nowhere. Putting on the brakes—even spending some time apart—is hard, but it is less emotionally

exhausting and brings all sorts of benefits. Taking things nice and easy, we have time to really get to know our loved one, to discover their past, their pleasures, their likes and dislikes, failings and charms, wants and needs. Old-fashioned courting at a gentle pace helps us be sure that we truly do go together like a horse and carriage.

puppy love

Love is nothing if not dogged. It will trot at our heels unnervingly, like a stray mongrel that attaches itself to us in the streets, then follows us home, to sit on the steps for days on end, head cocked quizzically on one side, eyes beseeching. By some strange sixth sense, some innate conviction, it knows it has found its rightful owner. How long will we hold out?

always and everywhere

Is there anywhere where love is not? Wherever it has been forced out it will always be struggling to find a way back. It will chip away tirelessly at a rock, with forgiveness its chisel and faith its mallet, to release the love that is captive within. It is easy to see love in beauty, in plenty; it is almost tangible, audible, in soaring cathedrals, in waterfalls, in symphonies, in radiant freckled faces. Yet love is everywhere if we look for it. In outer space, where the astronaut gazes down at the earth in awe. On the ocean bed, where the diver finds last letters scribbled in a sunken submarine. In a world where we often feel powerless to help where others are suffering, love makes us powerful. Like a butterfly flapping its wings in Brazil can cause a tornado in Texas, the love of one individual can lead to astonishing things.

pure and selfless

"Full many a flower is born to blush unseen," but love not returned is never wasted. It stays forever secret and pure, selfless in its giving, adding to the sum total of love in the world. It is the self-effacing love that puts the loved one first and desires their happiness above all—even when they choose to find it with someone else. Pressed between the pages of the heart, it is preserved in all its delicate beauty, giving off the faintest of fragrances that is more evocative than the echo of a mandolin.

one to one

Do two become one in the intimacy of love? Exquisitely. Yet in such a way that there is no diminishment, rather an enrichment. Minds and bodies intermingle and fuse to form a perfect whole of two complementary halves, each with its own integrity yet transfigured when paired with the other. When two souls unite, perhaps they resemble two rare pearls fashioned into a pair of earrings; each makes a statement when worn singly but together they are beyond compare. Both become even more themselves, at the same time realizing, with wonderment, that the other is "more myself than I am."

enduring love

To love is to lay ourselves bare to lacerating loss. How can we survive the gaping hole of grief? We go beyond tears, wading through sinking-sand days, awake through suffocating nights. All seems absence, nothingness. We chase a familiar head in the street but a stranger's face turns at our hope-dashed touch. Lilacs stir buried memories and every clock tells "the endless time of never coming back." To go on living seems callous,

unbearable, a betrayal. Yet incredibly, impossibly, there can be a slow awakening. A tiny blade of grass pokes through the frozen earth. Our love endures, connecting us like a rope of golden silk; we no longer see the other who is holding the opposite end, they have slipped into the next room, but we can still send ripples of love along it and feel them return. Slowly, for our loved one's sake, we can turn again to life and smile.

simply the best

Love is easily pleased. It does not need fireworks and fancy footwork, a diamond tiara or tons of mascara. Love is as happy with a cheese and pickle sandwich as with caviar served on a silver salver. Chopsticks and Chopin sound equally wondrous to love, if both are played with feeling. Love is two quietly waiting their turn, not a crowd that is pushing and shoving. It values the nonentity as much as the celebrity. Love is blinded by bright lights but sees lights that hide under bushels. Love can be lost in a bustling street but found on a deserted beach. It is grateful for a gorgeous bouquet but treasures a hand-picked posy and is especially fond of wallflowers. It tends not to shout from a soapbox but stammers in a still, small voice. A long-winded saga can blow love's mind but a three-line haiku melts its heart. The essence of love is simplicity.

brave heart

Choosing love is not a soft option. Love is frequently hard and has to be worked at. It takes dedication and application, perseverance and forbearance. It does not always come naturally. Love knows the need to be sometimes cruel to be kind, but it suffers as much as we do and shares our burden of pain. Sometimes we may have to face up to the truth that what we thought was love was really an infatuation, a yearning for someone unattainable who will never return our affections. Loving takes courage, courage to ask the difficult question and act on the right, not the easy, answer. Love does not shrink from self-denial, from holding back when going ahead would bring hurt and heartache to others. "They that have power to hurt and will do none" are graduates of the school of love.

the rainbow effect

If love is focused fiercely on a single point, if all our energies, emotions, thoughts, and hopes are trained on just one person, it can become like a blinding ray searing through a shard of glass to set a heap of tinder twigs on fire, leaving only charred remains. Better by far that love be a beam of sunlight streaming through a prism, radiating out on the other side in a rainbow of vibrant affections that enrich all those they rest on.

an awfully big adventure

"Feel the fear but do it anyway" applies to love as to so much in life. To shrink from the adventure of love is like being given a stunning, brand-new bicycle, then keeping it locked up in the garage in cellophane, creeping in now and then to gaze on it but never wheeling it out. We will never know that unforgettable moment of cycling for the first time, as exciting as first love.

Sometimes the effort of keeping a relationship going can be an uphill struggle, but the sense of achievement and relief when we succeed makes it all worthwhile. Some people seem to get the hang of love right away; others need stabilizers for a while. Most of us fall off a few times. Yet, once we have found we can do it, there is so much fun to be had—especially on a bicycle built for two.

the kiss of love

Will we be silent or speaking, laughing or crying when love appears? Will we be dancing or darning, smiling or frowning? Will it sparkle in a dewdrop, whistle with the lark, drift down on a dandelion fairy? Will it be in a look, a voice, a walk, a scent? The one thing required of us is that we realize this is the all-important moment. That we do not stir until we sense that it has us in its thrall, entirely, enchantingly. And then to respond in a way that is worthy of this wondrous gift. To feel our heart opening to receive and give, and in that split second begin to live.

perfect moment

Being in love can be numbing. We can give all we have to give and it won't be enough. We can slide into resenting our lover and be baffled by how we came to fall in love with someone who seems so alien. And then one night we will be dancing cheek to cheek, closer than close yet worlds apart. And the lights will suddenly go off with a bang. We cling to each other in the total darkness, wondering if this is the end. Our whole past together flashes before our eyes, the magical moments relived on fast forward. But then the lights go on again, and we are laughing and kissing and clutching each other. And, looking in each other's eyes, we realize that, all the while we were grumbling and thinking the grass to be greener elsewhere, we were failing to see that everything we wanted, our very best friend, was the person right beside us.

reach for the stars

It is not rocket science; it is both simpler and more stratospheric. Love is the ultimate in space exploration. It is the art of reaching for the stars while keeping our feet on the ground. It involves a union more awe-inspiring than a shuttle docking with a space station, but also a sensitive working out of how to orbit each other, giving a lover personal space and time to be themselves. We exist in a parallel universe all to ourselves. Sometimes our love can seem eclipsed by worries, sorrows or someone else, yet we always have the choice to hope and wait for the darkness to pass. We can hold on to our faith that although we may see only the tiniest crescent of our love, it has not, in fact, disappeared and in a little while the whole luminous moon of it will shine upon us again. Then we will have once more that lift-off feeling we had in those first levitating months of love when the earth moved.

First published by MQ Publications Limited
12 The Ivories, 6–8 Northampton Street
London N1 2HY

Copyright © 2003 MQ Publications Limited

TEXT COPYRIGHT © 2003 **libby willis**
DESIGN CONCEPT: **balley design associates**

ISBN: 0-7407-3869-0

Library of Congress Control Number: 2003103014